Everyday Reactions

by Lisa Oram

PEARSON
Scott Foresman

What You Already Know

Matter can change in many ways. A physical change causes matter to change the way it looks. But it does not change the kind of matter. A banana undergoes a physical change when it is sliced. A whole banana and a sliced banana are both bananas. Slicing the fruit caused a physical change.

One special physical change is a change in the state of the matter. There are three states of matter: liquid, solid, and gas. Liquid water freezes into ice. It changes from a liquid to a solid. Liquid water and ice are just different forms of the same kind of matter.

A chemical change causes one kind of matter to change into another kind of matter. When wood is burned, it becomes ash and smoke. Ash is not wood. Ash cannot become wood again. Burning caused a chemical change.

When two or more kinds of matter are combined, they can form a mixture. Mixtures are not a new kind of matter. Their ingredients can be separated. Salad is a mixture of several kinds of vegetables.

A solution is a kind of mixture in which one or more substances dissolve in another. Lemonade powder mixed with water forms a solution. The powder dissolves in water.

Many other changes in everyday life are pretty amazing. How does soap get you clean? How does food make you strong? This book explores how these everyday reactions work.

A salad is a mixture of vegetables.

Reactions All Around

Have you ever used a cold pack on a sprained ankle? One kind of cold pack must be kept in the freezer to stay cold. Another kind of cold pack just needs a squeeze to become cold.

When you squeeze this kind of pack, the substances inside mix together. One of them is water. The other is a chemical called ammonium nitrate. A reaction takes place when they are mixed together. This reaction takes in heat. Then the pack feels cold.

Hot packs also take advantage of a reaction involving heat. Instead of ammonium nitrate, they are filled with either calcium chloride or magnesium sulfate. Both substances release heat when mixed with water.

cold pack

cement

A chemical reaction takes place when cement is made.

What about preparing cement to build a brick wall? Cement begins as a dry powder. Mixing it with water forms a paste, which is spread between the bricks. A reaction takes place. The paste dries to form a strong, solid material.

These reactions show the difference between a physical change and a chemical change. Adding water to cold and hot packs changes the temperature but not the materials involved. It causes a physical change. Adding water to cement changes the materials involved. It causes a new kind of matter to form, which is a chemical change. Chemical changes require chemical reactions. Chemical reactions take place around us every day.

Filling Up

Chemical reactions even take place in the kitchen. For example, the heat of an oven can turn a mixture of ingredients into bread.

Bread starts out as a dough mixture that includes yeast and sugar. When yeast uses sugar for food, a chemical reaction takes place. This reaction produces carbon dioxide gas and alcohol as waste products. Kneading, or pressing, the dough makes it stringy and stretchy. Then the dough can trap the gas bubbles that are made by the yeast and sugar reaction.

The dough rests after kneading. During that time, carbon dioxide bubbles fill the dough. Then it becomes light and spongy. Baking is the final step before you can eat the bread.

Baking bread involves chemical reactions.

dough after rising

kneaded dough

baked loaf

dough mixture

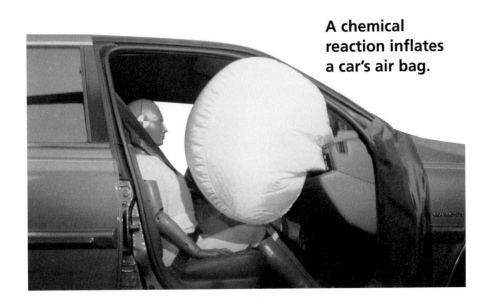

A chemical reaction inflates a car's air bag.

When a car's air bag opens, it fills with gas just like bread. Two chemicals are inside the air bag system. They are called sodium azide and potassium nitrate.

When a car stops suddenly, a sensor inside the steering wheel generates an electrical current. This causes a spark, which ignites the sodium azide. The sodium azide reacts with the potassium nitrate to form a gas called nitrogen. This is a very powerful reaction. The nitrogen blasts into the air bag at a speed approaching 250 miles per hour, inflating the bag in an instant. Fortunately, the nitrogen moves out of the air bag quickly, and the car's passengers are able to move.

Burning Bright

A candle burns brightly when an upside-down jar is first placed on top of it.

The flame goes out when the oxygen in the jar is used up.

Most people enjoy burning candles or sitting near a roaring campfire. But fire must be controlled. It can be very dangerous. What causes fire?

Fuel and oxygen combine in a chemical reaction called combustion. Many different substances can be fuel for a fire. Wax, wood, and paper are all examples. Oxygen is a gas found in the air. When oxygen and fuel are mixed and heated to a high temperature, they will combust. Combustion is burning. When something burns, it is very hot.

Smothering a fire with foam will block oxygen from reaching it.

Once a fire has started, it can grow quickly. As long as there is fuel and oxygen around, the fire will continue burning. To stop a fire, the fuel, heat, or oxygen must be taken away.

There are different ways to put out a fire depending on the fuel source that is burning. If trees are cleared from around a forest fire, the fire will not have enough fuel. Spraying cool water onto the fuel source will lower the heat of a fire. And smothering a fire with water or foam will block oxygen. Firefighters use foam to cover materials that are no longer burning so they do not catch fire again.

Coming Clean

We would all be dirty without the chemistry of soap. Soap and water react in a way that makes it possible for us to wash dirt off ourselves or other surfaces.

soap

The particles of soap are long. One end of a soap particle is attracted to dirt and grease. This end surrounds any dirt on a surface, such as your hands. The other end of the soap particle is attracted to the particles of running water. The end of the soap particle that attracts dirt is also pulled toward the water particles. The attraction between the soap and water particles lifts dirt right off the surface. The running water then carries soap and dirt away.

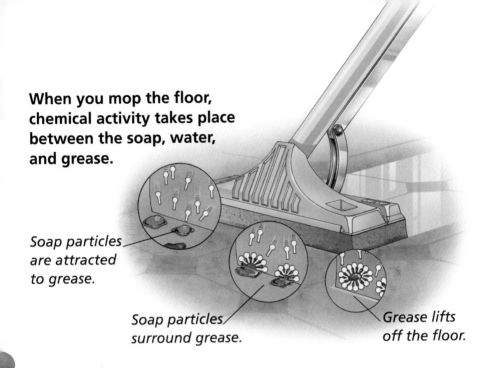

When you mop the floor, chemical activity takes place between the soap, water, and grease.

Soap particles are attracted to grease.

Soap particles surround grease.

Grease lifts off the floor.

Detergents work much like soap does to remove dirt from clothing. Stains, however, can be hard to remove. It's even harder when the stain particles and the fabric are similar. It's also hard if the stain, such as a grass stain, has been rubbed in below the surface.

To fight stains, some detergents include chemicals that get stains out of clothing. These stain removers cause a chemical reaction with the stain. The stain particles change. This allows the stain particles to separate from the fabric.

Some fabrics, such as polyester and nylon, do not stain as easily. Their particles are different. The stain has a harder time attaching to the fabric.

Digesting Food

Have you ever thought about what happens to food after you eat it?

Many chemical reactions take place in your body to digest food. Digestion is the process of breaking down food into tiny particles. Then the particles can travel throughout your body. This is how you get the vitamins and minerals you need.

Digestion begins in your mouth. Chemicals called enzymes start to break down food. Enzymes in your intestine break down food even more. Your stomach also produces hydrochloric acid, which turns food into a liquid paste. It also helps kill bacteria that may enter your stomach with food.

The acid in your stomach is needed for digestion. But too much acid can make your stomach hurt. People take medicines called antacids when they have too much stomach acid.

Sodium bicarbonate, or baking soda, is a common ingredient in antacids. It is the opposite of an acid. It is called a base. Bases react with acids to cancel out the effect of the acid. This process is called neutralization. When an acid and a base interact, they are neutralized.

Pickling in vinegar kills bacteria, which is also what the acid in your stomach does.

Indigestion Remedies

If you want to see how an acid and a base work together, sprinkle some baking soda on a lemon. The fizzing you see is the acid and the base producing carbon dioxide gas. The gas is not an acid or a base. It is neutral.

Fizzing occurs as powder reacts with juice.

Battery Action

Batteries are everywhere. There are different kinds of batteries for different uses. Can you think of some things that use battery power? You might have thought about a camera, a flashlight, or a cell phone.

A battery is a container full of chemicals. All batteries have a positive and negative end, or terminal. A wire can connect these two terminals. When the terminals are connected, chemicals inside the battery react. The chemicals react to form electricity. This is called an electrochemical reaction. The electricity will travel from one terminal to another. Then the camera, flashlight, or cell phone will work.

Battery-operated toy car

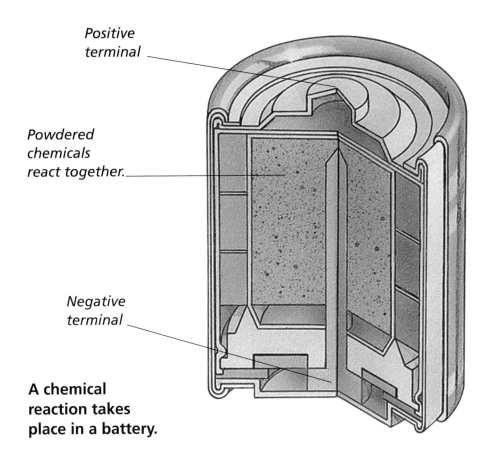

Positive terminal

Powdered chemicals react together.

Negative terminal

A chemical reaction takes place in a battery.

When you want to listen to music, you simply turn on the radio. When you eat breakfast, your body gets energized for the day. The chemistry in your life is mostly invisible. But chemical reactions cause changes. These changes allow us to drive cars and use electrical appliances. They cause metal to rust, leaves to change their colors, fireflies to light up at night, and much more. Chemical reactions are an amazing part of life!

Glossary

antacid   a substance that cancels out the effects of an acid

chemistry   the science of matter, what it's made of, and how it changes

combustion   the chemical reaction of burning

digestion   the process that breaks down food in the body

electrochemical reaction   a reaction that creates electricity

enzymes   chemicals in the body that help with digestion

neutralization   the reaction between an acid and a base that creates a neutral substance